ANKER

BATTERY

GUIDE

JAMES

CHRISTIANSEN

TABLE OF CONTENTS

INTRODUCTION

As it is, living in the world that is being constantly modified by technological advancement to the extent that it has directly affected nearly every aspect of our lifestyle, we are also in the position of working constantly, whether that's taking work home or managing our household duties. As such, functionality and efficiency are on-demand requirements of the present day reality.

At any given time, we usually find ourselves in need of some sort of need to be connected online in order to manage our lives whether its paying our bills or checking if our boss has emailed a new task to us. Our portable electronic devices are the answer we have to all these necessities. Therefore, it is absolutely necessary to stay connected to our portable electronic gadgets and this is simply not possible without keeping them charged. Just as we need a breath of life in us to stay alive, these devices need a charge all of the time. Without a charge, they are dead, and their death means virtual death for us.

Here's where Anker's 2nd generation of Astro series and 40W 5-Port Family-Sized Desktop USB charger come in to help you maintain seamless connectivity with your electronic gadgets. Of course, there are a number of other chargers on the market which are also good. But there are reasons for recommending Anker products above other competing products, and we are going to look into those reasons in the following chapters.

Normally, when you are out to buy a battery charger, at the back of your mind is the consideration of your needs. There are several factors to be considered. You know well what the battery of the device you are using demands. And the speed with which the external battery charger charges your device is also important for you.

Then, there is a question of the design and life of the external battery pack. You may like the design and speed of some batteries; but, then, it may be so that they have a shorter battery life than other batteries which may not look good but have am acceptable speed and longer life span.

Since its first market appearance, Anker has been known to have attended well to such details. Not only in case of the external battery packs, but also regarding other products, Anker's constant endeavor has been to contribute to healthy competition in the market of electronic gadgets through constant and excellent increment in its product line that includes batteries and chargers, along with cases and protectors, key boards and mice, and connectivity products. This guide presents a comprehensive survey of their external battery packs, bringing out their virtues in a somewhat detailed manner.

The products dealt with here include the Anker 2nd Gen Astro 6000 mAh (2A Output) Portable Charger External Battery Pack with Power IQ Technology, Anker 2nd Gen Astro E3 Dual-Port Ultra Compact External Battery Portable USB Charger Power Bank with Power IQ Technology, Anker Astro E5 15000 mAh Dual USB Portable Charger Ultra-High Density External Battery Pack, Anker Astro Mini 3000 mAh Ultra-Compact Lipstick-Sized Portable External Battery Power Bank with Power IQ Technology, and Anker 40W 5-Port Family-Sized Desktop USB Charger with Power IQ Technology.

As mentioned above, this guide endeavors to inform you about why external charging devices are a must and why these Anker products are recommended more than other devices available in the market. This exercise is necessary to put you in the position where you can make an informed choice of an external battery charger.

ANKER ASTRO 6000 MAH (2A OUTPUT) PORTABLE CHARGER EXTERNAL BATTERY PACK WITH POWER IQ TECHNOLOGY

The Astro 6000 mAh (2A Output) portable charger external battery pack is very elegant with its sturdy plastic body lined with soft rubber.

This battery is designed especially for you if you need to travel frequently, and, while in transit, make use of your smartphone or tablet for a long duration. This is because its size perfectly suits the size of your pocket, having the dimension of just 93x46x25 mm and weighing just 134 gm. It can easily be held in your palm. But when it comes to performance, it is so efficient that you will hardly feel the absence of an AC power source in its presence.

Anker Astro 6000 mAh helps you save your Portable Electronic Devices from getting crippled without power – portable devices such as iPhone 5S, 5C, 5, 4S, iPad Air, mini, Galaxy S5, S4, S3, Note 3, Galaxy Tab 3, 2, Nexus

4, 5, 7, 10, HTC One, One 2 (M8), MOTO X, G, LG Optimus, PS Vita, and other smartphones and tablets. All you need to do to charge your device is to connect it with the battery pack with an appropriate cable. As soon as your device is connected with the battery, it starts getting charged automatically.

Making use of Lithium battery technology, this battery packs 6000 mAh power and is endowed with a smart USB port for any Android or Apple device, a micro USB battery charging port offering 1 A speed to charge the battery. This battery can be recharged 500 times. It does not come with an AC wall charger but it is to be charged with 5 VDC at 1 Amp, and takes 5 to 6 hours' time to get fully charged. The USB port is "smart" in that it feeds your electronic device just as much as it is capable of eating – no more, no less.

Another very interesting feature this battery offers is the 10 LED lights – each representing 10% capacity – in front to indicate the charge status of the battery as it is being used or charged. All you have to do to know the charge status of the battery is to shake it. The LED ring will light up to show you the charge status. This is one of the features that make this battery score an advantage over most of the other batteries which have 4 LEDs, each of which is showing 25% of the total charge of the battery. In showing a 10% increase in charge, this Astro gives a more precise reading of the charge status.

It is seen in practice that the actual capacity of the external battery is always less than it is claimed to be in advertisements. This is another point where Astro 6000 mAh (2A Output) marks a distinction because, thanks to its efficient control circuit and high-quality cells, it offers 80% efficiency in actual performance.

Now if you compare other products with this Astro, you will discover that the efficiency of this Anker product is 15% higher than the average of 35% that the industry has to offer. Thus, you expect 4700-4800 mAh of charging power from an Astro 6000 mAh (2A output). The Romoss Sofun 5200 External Battery Pack, for instance, comes very cheap and has some of the features that the Astro 6000 mAh has. But it lacks the capacity that Astro has, and its output is also less. So even with its 81% efficiency, it cannot fully charge such devices as iPad 3 or 4. The RAV Power Luster 6000 mAh Backup External Battery Pack Power Bank Charger costs more and seems to outdo the Astro 6000 mAh with the features it offers. But, actually, it does not – or rather it cannot. If we study both the products more closely, we realize how great the difference is between the two.

The RAVPowers Luster 6000 mAh measures 3.9x1.6x0.8 inches and weighs 5.05 ounces. In other words, it is larger in size and greater in weight than Anker. However, it little affects its portability. You can carry it wherever you want to. And it offers 6000 mAh power, a built-in flashlight, a greater Output (5V 2.1 A), and requires a greater Input (5V 1.5A) than this Anker battery. What is good about it is that it automatically shuts down in case there is a short circuit or sudden power fluctuation. Also, it shuts down automatically a few seconds after you unplug your device. And it can charge all devices that an Anker battery can. So far, so good. The real difference between the two becomes apparent once you use them.

It starts with the design. The Anker battery has absolutely no button! It only has the Input and Output slots. To set it to go, all you have to do is to give it a shake. The moment it starts, again it marks another point of departure – for the better – from its nearest rival. The shake given to it lights the 10 LED lights to show the power that is left in the battery. RAV offers only 4 LEDs to show the charge status. As mentioned above regarding its 10 LEDs, this Astro 6000 mAh offers a more precise charge status reading than the RAVPower Luster 6000mAh.

Another thing is that there is no power button in the Anker battery. The moment you plug your device into it, it starts to charge your device. And when you unplug your device, it stops automatically. Here's where a problem lies in RAV. Its power button is situated in such a place, and it is such that there is all the possibility it gets pressed accidentally and easily in your pocket to start it. The result is power loss. Not only that, it has been observed in actual performance that RAV has a shorter battery life than the Anker Astro 2nd generation 6000 mAh battery. And it also takes a considerably longer time to get charged.

There is another product, the AYL 2nd Gen 6000 mAh (2.1A Output), which seems to come closer to matching its strength with this Astro device from Anker. It comes cheap, offers a two years warranty (!) and greater output; but, again, in actual practice it has proved to be quite inefficient, and fails to make true the claims made for it.

Another point on which other competitors do not stand a comparison with this Anker product is the loss of power that external battery packs are known to suffer. This happens because of voltage conversion and circuit resistance. The Astro 2nd generation batteries are no exception to that – including the battery under consideration here. They also tend to lose 20% of their total power, of which 6% is lost due to the heating up of the circuit and voltage conversion, and 14% because of the charging cable and the device you charge with it. It would be relevant here to inform you that the Astro 6000 mAh does not heat up above the room temperature when used.

Thus, though the Astro 6000 mAh (2A Output) portable charger is diminutive in size, it hides tremendous power that lasts longer than many of its market competitors.

If you're interested in taking a closer look at the Anker Astro battery pack, simply scan the code below to view it on Amazon:

ANKER 2ND GENERATION ASTRO E3 DUAL-PORT ULTRA-COMPACT PORTABLE USB CHARGER WITH POWER IQ TECHNOLOGY

The Anker 2nd generation Astro E3, a Lithium Polymer type battery, looks great with its sleek black finish. It's a dual-port USB charger power bank which boasts broad compatibility Power IQ technology, which makes it an absolutely fast and high capacity charger.

If you buy a 2nd generation Astro E3, what you find contained in this battery package is the Astro E3 external battery itself, accessories, a user manual, and an 18-month warranty. You have to purchase Apple adapters and a Samsung 30-pin adapter separately. It is recommended that you make use of your device's original cable, a third-party certified cable like MFI, or the cable included in the package. The micro USB cable that comes with the package works perfectly with Samsung Galaxy S5, Note 3 .and other micro USB 3.0 devices.

What is new about this 2nd generation Astro is that its recharge rate is increased from 1.5A to 2A, reducing its recharge time by 25%. Thus, with a 2A adapter this battery now takes about 6 hours to recharge. Here's where it surpasses its nearest rival, namely, Jackery Giant.

Jackery Giant offers 10,400 mAh power (which is more than what the Anker battery offers); three ports, two USB ports (one port offering 5V/1V Amp and another 5V/2.1 Amp Output), and one micro USB port for either charging this external battery or any micro USB compatible device; and two LED flashlights. Just like the Anker battery, Jackery Giant also turns off automatically when a device is fully charged. But the problem is that it takes as long as 10 hours to recharge. And, by the way, it is a bit odd, but this battery features three LEDs to indicate its charge status.

Just like Jackery Giant, the Lenmar PowerPort Wave also offers 11000 mAh power and three USB ports, enabling it to charge most of the mobile devices for about four times and an iPad for one time. But it is quite heavy, and takes very long to get charged even with a 2.1A charger.

Returning to the 2nd generation Astro E3, it holds as good as a 10,000 mAh capacity which enables it to recharge almost anything – whether it is iPhone 5s, 5c, 5; iPad Air mini; Galaxy S5, S4; Tab 2; Note 3, 2; LG G3; Nexus; HTC One M8; MOTO X; PS Vita; or many other devices which are USB-charged. It is practically proven that it can charge iPhones for more than four times and high capacity devices like Galaxy S4 for more than twice. What it does not support is the iPod nano, Asus tablets, the LG G2, and certain GPS and Bluetooth devices.

But the most important feature of the Astro E3 is its Power IQ technology. What the Power IQ technology actually does is to enhance the compatibility of this battery. It has been observed that not all ports of a charging device, which is not featuring Power IQ technology, are made alike. Only the standard ports of such batteries are able to effectively support devices such as Android and Apple. But this compromises their recharge rate.

For example, there is the Lumsing 11000 mAh portable battery. Just like the Jackery Giant, it contains more power than the Anker battery, and offers as many as five USB ports, each of which haves a different output capacity. You can use them simultaneously, but you have to be able to count their output capacity and your device's input requirement. You can't just use any port for any device you like. This, indeed, is by no means a convenient system.

The advantage this Astro gains over such chargers by having Power IQ technology is that each of its port is able to identify your device to render it compatible with its charging requirements, and that too without compromising the charging speed. To put it more specifically, this charger can charge any Android, Apple, or any other device at the speed of about 3 Amps overall and 3 Amps per port.

It's 5.39x2.64x0.65 inch dimensions and just 8.64 ounce weight lend - it superb portability. It has greater portability than its rivals. You can carry it with you wherever you go in a hassle-free manner. Apart from looks and portability, what is special about its design is that it aims to be functional. It offers 5V / 2A input, and uses a 2A adapter for fastest charge time, that is, 6 hours. Yes, it scores its success through its efficiency. It has 500+ lifetime charge cycles. It is given 4 LEDs to indicate the charge status of the battery.

Here, it will avail you to know that in order for your battery's life to last longer, you must charge and recharge it at least once in 3 to 4 months. Most external batteries are known to have static power consumption below 100uA. It means that they are depleted in a time which ranges between 3.5 to 20 years if they are not used for these many years. However, the li-ion battery will not take more than 2 years to drain. Another thing you need to know is that you must not over-charge or over-discharge it. Ideally, it is to be kept charged between 5% and 95%.

Finally, what we can fairly say on behalf of this 2nd generation Astro E3 is that it does not derive credit from the name "Anker" for the prestige it holds the way products like Sony 10,000 mAh USB extended battery pack power bank CP-F2L and CP-F10L do. The one advantage that both of these Sony batteries seem to have, above anything else, is that they bear the brand "Sony." Sony's reputation is the only thing which would entice anyone to buy these products, which have utterly failed to live up to their name. The Anker battery, compared to the above named Sony devices, succeeds by its efficiency.

Indeed, the Anker 2nd generation Astro E3 is a real good device to have. It is sure to keep you connected with life – if life means fun and functionality to you.

This battery can be seen in greater detail on Amazon by scan the code below:

Have you found this book useful so far? I certainly hope so and if you've found even one or two helpful tips or tricks, I'd really appreciate it if you could leave a short review of the book on Amazon which can be done by scanning this code.

Thanks so much!!!

ANKER ASTRO MINI 3000 MAH ULTRA-COMPACT LIPSTICK-SIZED EXTERNAL BATTERY POWER BANK

The Anker Astro Mini 3000 mAh is an external battery power bank with Power IQ technology, and you are bound to find it easy on the eye. It is truly one of those small things which make big things happen. If in doubt, try it!

It belongs to the Anker Astro Series that has emerged as the most favored product among the external battery pack users. The reasons for the success of this series and its popularity are quite obvious, and the Astro Mini 3000 mAh amply illustrates them.

The very first reason is the size of this ultra-compact portable charger. It is the size of a lipstick, having the dimensions of 3.5x0.9x0.9 inches, and weighing no more than 80 gm. Its extraordinary portability is at your disposal at any time in any place. What is impressive about its design is that all its important active elements stay well-protected inside its aluminum outer cover. So you do not have to worry about your device getting damaged very easily. This small device is quite strong.

Returning to the portability of a device, if we compare products competing with the Astro Mini 3000 mAh (priced at $19.99) we find that it is not the only product which impresses us by its looks and size and portability. For instance, there are also the TeckNet Power Bank Mini 3000 mAh USB External Battery Pack (priced at $12.97 £11.99), the Veho Pebble Mini 3000 mAh portable battery pack (priced at $28.43 £13.95), and the RAVPower Luster Mini 3000 mAh external battery pack Power Bank charger (priced at $17.99 £10.99), etc., which are almost the same size and shape, and not weighing much either. So we may fairly say that if we are to find Astro's excellence, we find it in its technical and functional elements. Easy portability is just one of its selling points.

The Astro Mini 3000 mAh thrives on Samsung Grade A cells and microchips. These ensure reliability and safety. You can charge this device in 3 to 4 hours with the help of an AC 0.8 amp adapter. However, this adapter does not come with the pack. All that the pack includes is the Anker Astro Mini 3000 mAh External Battery, Micro USB cable, travel pouch, welcome guide, and 18-month warranty.

The USB port, micro-USB port, and power button to start the device are all placed on the rear end of the battery. The auto cut off feature of the device is quite impressive, in that it saves the battery from getting self-discharged when it is not in use.

With this tiny device, you can charge such devices as the iPhone 5S, 5C, 5, 4S, Galaxy S5, S4, S3, Note 3, Nexus 4, HTC One, One 2 (M8), Nokia Lumia 520, 1020, and most other smartphones. What this battery cannot support is the iPod Nano, Samsung Tab2, Asus tablets, LG G2, and some GPS and Bluetooth devices. And if you are charging your iPhone or Samsung Galaxy S5 with it, you can charge it fully. Thus, you can have 7 hours talk time if you are using the iPhone and 70+ hours of audio playback on the Galaxy S5 or on any other devices. So as regards its efficiency and capacity, it will not be wrong to compare it with an ant which can lift a weight which is 5000 times more than its body weight. And as for its efficiency, the book of Proverbs in the Bible speaks enough of it in a small space when it exhorts a lazy fellow to follow its example.

The real advantage that this Astro has is its Power IQ technology which optimizes the compatibility of this battery pack to accommodate with Android, Apple, and other devices by enabling a charge speed of up to about 1 Amp. It is this Power IQ technology which is the unique selling point of Anker products, giving them their real identity. Another impressive element of this battery is that it automatically supplies the power that your device requires.

However, this Astro is lacking in some respects when compared to two other external batteries, namely, the MyCharge Summit 3000 and the Innergie PocketCell. It has to be turned off when the charging is complete. It does not turn off automatically. And there are also some very impressive features in the Summit 3000 which the Astro battery does not have. For instance, Summit accommodates several different types of cables for input and output. It also contains a surprise element in the form of a speaker which, with its voice and tone modes alerts you concerning the time that you should plug or unplug your device and about how much power is left. Apart from this feature, you also have the LED indicators to inform you about the charge status of the battery.

Not only that, it also has a system which enables it to decide for itself about the needs of which of the three devices it charges simultaneously is to be prioritized. However, it shares with the Astro Mini 3000 mAh the weakness of not turning off automatically when charging is complete. The Innergie PocketCell does not go so far in the wrong direction when we compare it with the MyCharge Summit 3000 and the Anker Astro Mini 3000 mAh. This is because it turns off ten minutes after the charging is complete. It means that the prospect of wasting the power of the battery is not very serious.

Having said this, we have to say that for the price tag attached to the Anker Astro Mini 3000 mAh, we have no right to expect more than it is expected to do for our devices. And the fact is that it does perform for your devices what the above mentioned batteries can and that too at a far cheaper rate. Just look at the price set on the products which are offering competition to this Astro!

Indeed, this Anker Astro Mini 3000 mAh is designed specifically to answer to your needs and serve all practical purposes for which you may require it.

If you're interested in learning more about the Anker Astro Mini, scanning this code below to view it on Amazon:

ANKER ASTRO E5 15000 MAH DUAL USB PORTABLE CHARGER

The Anker Astro E5 15000 mAh, an ultra-high density external battery pack, is a power in black/white featuring dual USB ports, one of which offers 1A/5V and the other 2A/5V, a built-in flashlight, and 4 LEDs each of which indicating 25% of the total charge.

The Astro E5 15000 mAh is said to be the world's most compact external battery, having the dimensions of 4.9x3x0.9 inches and weighing but 316 gm. Apart from the compactness, the big plus of this battery pack is the advantage of long lasting power that it offers.

If you visit any ecommerce site to compare the different products available in the market for you, what you find is that there are a number of other products which offer features similar to those that the Astro E5 15000 mAh offers. Indeed, some of them seem even more impressive than this Anker product. What's more, some of them are even cheaper than this Astro, which costs $39.99 £37.99.

For instance, there is the EasyAcc 15600 mAh high capacity 2A input power bank built-in dual LED flashlight dual USB external charger which costs just $39.99, the Innori 15000 mAh dual USB backup universal power bank external battery pack portable power pack charger costing but $38.99, the RAVPower 15000 mAh portable power bank pack external battery charger costing $59.99, the Henweit power bank 15000 mAh USB external battery costing just $30.24, and so on. But one thing that you notice is that there are far fewer takers for these products than this Astro. It not only reflects the trust that the external battery buyers have in the Anker battery but also suggests a lot about its performance in practice.

Coming to the battery itself, it works greatly for the iPad Air, Mini, iPhone 5S, 5C, 4S, Galaxy S5, S4, S3, Note 3, Nexus 4, 5, 7, 10, HTC One, One 2 (M8), Motorola Droid, LG Optimus, MOTO X, and many other USB-charged devices requiring 5V input. All you have to do to tap its power for your devices is to press the charge button once. If you press it twice, what you get is the flash-light going. Another thing that you need to know is that this battery does not support Samsung, Asus tablets, iPod nano, and certain GPS and Bluetooth devices.

The Astro E5 15000 mAh boasts 5V / 3A total output through dual USB ports (5V / 3A and 5V / 1A). These ports allow you to charge two devices at the same time, and at high speed whether you are charging your iPad, iPhone, Android, or any other device with it.

With the 15000 mAh power that it packs, you can charge your iPhone about 7 times, and phones like the Galaxy S4 having high capacity about 4 times. But if you charge devices such as the iPad 3 / 4, which has the 11560 mAh battery, then what you notice is that the battery pack suffers energy loss due to self-discharge, voltage conversion, and circuit resistance – the factors which work in a combined manner to consume 20% of the total charge. Nevertheless, Astro E5 does charge such devices fully. That is something; for so many of its market competitors fail to perform when it comes to charging a device like the iPad 3 or 4.

If you buy the Astro E5, you get a micro USB cable for charging the battery, a travel pouch, and an instructional manual along with the battery. The package does not include a cable for charging Apple devices, for they are to be charged with the cable which comes with those devices. Though it is not included in the pack, it is highly recommended that you use a 5V / 1.5A adapter for the fastest charging time, which is about 9 to 10 hours.

Indeed, you have a reason to buy the Astro E5 15000 mAh because the Astro E5 defies comparison when it comes to performance. Sure thing!

The Anker Astro E5 is a truly powerful battery solution; click on the picture below to find out more about it on Amazon:

ANKER 40W 5-PORT FAMILY-SIZED DESKTOP USB CHARGER WITH POWER IQ TECHNOLOGY

The Anker 40W 5-Port Family-Sized Desktop USB charger with Power IQ technology is undoubtedly one of the best offerings in the market, and sure enough, it is with its truly impressive features, and the advantage they offer for the users who choose to buy it. It guarantees lifetime reliability owing to the industrial-grade materials and premium circuitry used in it.

This 40W USB charger has a unibody design to enhance its portability. It is about the size of a deck of playing cards, having the dimensions of just 3.6x2.3x1.0 inches. And with its 100-240 V input, it should be making an obvious choice for you if you frequently travel abroad.

This charger is capable of charging any device, whether it is the iPhone 5s, 5c, 5 or iPad Air mini or Galaxy S5, S4 or Note 3, 2, or the new HTC One (M8) or Nexus. And, in case it fails to charge your device, check it out whether your device is USB-powered and has a voltage input of 5V. This is essential if you want to use this battery pack for charging your device. Also, see to it that you are making use of the original cable that came with your device in order to charge it.

You can charge as many as five devices at the same time, notwithstanding the battery type that they make use of. This is because this battery charger offers as many as 5 ports. However, you need to ensure that the input current of these devices do not exceed the limit of 8A.

Another thing is that you do not have to find out a specific port for charging a specific device of yours; because each and every port of this battery pack is capable of charging any device at maximum speed – thanks to the PowerIQ technology.

Like other PowerIQ technology enabled devices, the Anker 40W 5-Port Desktop USB charger works wonderfully well with Android, Apple, and other devices, enabling charging speed up to 8 Amps overall and 2.4 Amps per port.

Truly, there are not too many market competitors for this Anker battery. There are certain products like the Vinsic 5-Port 40W USB charger and the Bolse NewPower 40W (5V/8A) 5-Port USB Wall / Desktop charger, which do offer almost all the features that this Anker battery is offering, and yet they fail significantly in certain respects when they are compared with the Anker product which is under consideration. Following are the reasons why the Anker has been able to withstand competition. Let us first take the Vinsic 5-Port 40W USB Charger.

Vinsic offers 40W power and 5 Ports, enabling you to charge as many as five devices at the same time. It is compatible with all 5V USB charged devices like the iPad, iPhone, Samsung tab, etc. And its Smart Power technology enables it to identify the connected device and maximizes compatibility and charging speed (up to 2.4 Amps) for it. It is made of industrial-grade materials, and that this device can cope up with short-circuits and power fluctuations. In all these things, this device does bear resemblance with the specifications of the Anker battery. But, in fact, the Vinsic does not have UL (Underwriters Laboratories) certification. It is a mark of quality for electronic goods to have this certificate. It guarantees safety.

Now, if we turn to the Bolse NewPower 40W (5V/8A) 5-Port USB Wall / Desktop charger, we are faced with the claim that this battery is the world's first 5 port 5V/8A USB charger. This device too has a unibody and compact design, offering 5V/8A Output and 110-220V Input, and is guarded from short-circuit and power fluctuation. It has 5 ports of which two ports (each rated at 5V/2A) are for devices like the iPhone and iPad; one port (rated at 5V/2A) is specifically for a Samsung device; and two universal ports (each rated at 5V/1A) for any Apple or Android devices. All ports charge your different devices at full speed. But all the ports of this battery do not have what the Anker battery has. All the 5 ports of the Anker battery are universal and, therefore, each and every port of it is capable of charging any device. This is not all. The Bolse NewPower 40W (5V/8A) 5-Port USB Wall / Desktop charger suffers terribly from the way it is designed. Its ports are located on three different sides facing in three different directions. It is only when you try to use all the five ports of this battery to charge your devices that you realize how odd it is. The whole charging process literally gets messed up, or rather you get messed up with the charging process.

The Anker 40W 5-Port Desktop USB charger is not only nicely designed, it impresses us more with its functional elements. Undoubtedly, it is the best choice that you can make if you make use of more than one device.

Scan the code below to get more information about this great solution for battery needs; the link will take you to Amazon.

CONCLUSION

As stated in the introduction to this brief guide, this detailed survey of the new generation chargers rolled out by Anker is made for you - if you are one of those who know how important it is to stay connected with your portable devices at all times, no matter where you are.

And if you are one of those who have not yet realized this, you need only to think practically about how important sending one short but important SMS or MMS or email or brief telephone communication or such other ways of communication may turn out to be when the time comes. If your boss needs something at 7 PM on a Friday evening and you're out to dinner with a dead smartphone, that may not look so great to your boss when you don't reply to his email until Monday morning!

Let alone the importance of communication, sometimes even it is the processing of your data – whatever they may be – is the need of a moment. At times, even having a handy way of providing yourself some entertainment becomes an absolute necessity. You have to depend upon your portable device – whether it is a smartphone or a tablet or some other USB device – for any of the reasons given above.

And suppose your PED is dead on these occasions due to your failure to keep it charged? These Anker products reviewed in this guide are meant just for occasions like these.

The purpose of having gone the whole length to convince you about why the Anker products should practically hold preference over other competing products is to put you in the know of the fact that an Anker external battery pack of your choice is not just another way of helping you make the best use of your time and space, but it is THE BEST.

To check the veracity of this claim, all you have to do is to go online and visit any ecommerce portal and go through all the external battery chargers showcased out there, keeping one eye on the number of customer reviews they have attracted. Find out which product is having the maximum number of positive customer reviews. It tell-tales the trend among the external battery pack buyers. In fact, ANKER IS THE TREND!

This should boost your trust in Anker products. Having them on hand will ensure you that your devices will stay alive to serve you when you need them most. You no longer have to be at home or depend on your car for charging your devices. While going through the customer reviews on Amazon, I came across one very interesting review in which the reviewer came up with some really interesting results that he received on putting to the test the output capacity of the Anker 2nd generation Astro 6000 mAh (2A Output) portable charger using his Kindle Fire, 2 iPhones, and iPad. He practically proved that this battery has 83% efficiency which in and of itself is truly amazing. The conclusion of all his meticulous experiments with this particular product is that the Anker batteries do not let you down and are the best on the market today. It's as simple as that.

Thanks for reading this guide and I truly hope you've found it helpful! As always, I love to connect with my readers and you can find me on Twitter at @JChristBooks or contact me on email at the9cygul@gmail.com

Lastly, if you've enjoyed this book, I'd appreciate it if you could please leave a review of the book on Amazon which can be done by scanning this code

Thanks and good luck with your Anker batteries!

Sample From: "Amazon Prime Membership & Amazon Fire TV Box Set" by James Christiansen

INTRODUCTION

Prominent software companies like Microsoft, Google and Apple, have been exploring the realm of television for years. Traditional American families spend the majority of their leisure time watching television, and with the technological advances of smart phones and tablets computers, conventional television is constantly changing. There is an influx of streaming devices or set-top boxes capable of connecting to Wi-Fi system, via a USB port or Ethernet cable. These devices are able to deliver numerous live channels and videos on demand to the US market.

Cable television is becoming a thing of the past and technology relies heavily on the internet. People are watching television through DTH or IPTV (Internet Protocol Television), rather than using outdated cable television as the sole provider. Televisions are no longer passive devices limited to just being used for viewing pleasure, but have become interactive devices where you can play games and connect with other users. Exclusive gaming consoles such as Microsoft Xbox and Sony Playstation are still available to the consumer, but none includes Live Media Broadcasting or Streaming TV.

Amazon started as an online seller of books in 1994. Since that time the company has grown into one of the most dominant forces on the internet, and the largest global online retailer. In 2007, Amazon released the very first eBook reader: the Kindle. From there, the Kindle line has expanded to include both the Amazon Fire and the Fire HDX. These devices are tablets running Amazon's Android-based Fire OS. For the past two decades, Amazon has continued to expand their empire in impressive ways. Starting as a small bookstore, they have expanded to become a retail giant who in addition to manufacturing hardware, is also one of the leading providers of online streaming content. Launching Fire TV was just another extension of Amazon's ambitious legacy.

The growing demand for digital media provided the perfect platform for Amazon to branch out into, and they dived right in. In an estimated $70 billion TV market, Amazon overtook the competition and caught the attention of consumers'.

Peter Larsen, Amazon's Vice President, unveiled Fire TV on the 2nd of April 2014, during a high profile media event in New York. Rivaling the likes of illustrious Apple TV, Roku 3 and Google's ChromeCast with a host of unique features like gaming and voice search, Amazon is selling the Fire TV at the same price as the competition. Selling at $99 in the US market, the same price as Apple TV and Roku 3. Thanks to Fire TV, Amazon has officially entered the streaming battle that could decide the future of television.

The Fire TV system is a small black, box with a small remote control. The setup has been designed to be quick and user-friendly, to the point where an introductory video starts as soon as it is turned on. This feature gives users a virtual guide for its start up, how to use the apps as well as additional offers for the users. After the introduction, or should you skip it entirely, the Fire TV displays a variety of new movies and series in addition to the built in apps and games. The browsing option appears on the left hand side of the screen, so users are able to skim through specific categories using this feature. But if you don't know what you're looking for, you can just say it into the built-in microphone on the remote. This is a standout feature for the Amazon Fire TV, along with the gaming feature as well as ASAP (Advanced Search and Prediction).

Pushing the boundaries and thinking ahead helps Amazon create concepts like the Fire TV revolution. This has been a successful business strategy for the online empire and will continue to bring success as Amazon goes up against the likes of Google, Microsoft and Apple.

CHAPTER 1

WHAT IS AMAZON FIRE TV – FEATURES, PROS AND CONS

Rumors of Amazon working on a streaming media device circulated for a long time. This sparked interest and curiosity throughout the market that there could be an alternative to the former, cluttered streaming media market. It was reported that Apple TV had been well received after its launch, and the updated Roku 3 was considered to be the best app provider on the market. There was also a considerable fan following for Google's ChromeCast thanks to the simplicity of the system and cost effective price tag. But once Amazon launched their Fire TV in April 2014, they were official part of the streaming media domain.

Offering a bouquet of channels and videos along with a variety of apps and games that the user can play using a game controller. These controllers will need to be bought separately though.

Overall, it offers almost everything that the competing streaming devices have, with the exception of a few channels and apps. What sets Amazon apart is the trend setting, mid-level gaming experience that is included in the system. While it can't compete with high-end gaming consoles like Xbox or Play Station, it is still a groundbreaking system.

The interface has been described as "flat", because everything is laid out on one level. Although it doesn't offer the beautiful, tiered storefront that Apple TV does, Fire TV's arrangement is still as efficient and effective as any other digital media TV device.

Technical Specification:

- Processor: It has a 1.7Ghz Fast Quad-core Qualcomm Snapdragon 600
- RAM: It has a built-in memory of 2GB
- Storage: The internal storage is 8GB
- Ports: HDMI, Ethernet, USB
- Wireless: MIMO Dual-band, Dual-Antenna, 802.11 a/b/g/n, Bluetooth 4.0
- OS: Fire TV OS, based on Android 4.2.2 Jellybean
- GPU: Adreno 320 GPU for a great gaming experience
- Video Display: 1080p HD and Dolby Digital Plus Surround sound through HDMI Port.
- Remote: A simplified yet fully functional remote with no line of sight required. It connects via Bluetooth

The Quad-Core processor is another impressive feature of Fire TV, which is both responsive as well as powerful. Let's have a look at the positives that Fire TV has on offer:

The Pros

- The Fire TV box and remote come were designed with elegance in mind. The streamlined box and remote works through Bluetooth, and the remote control is similar to Apple TV's along with the directional wheel. As mentioned previously, the remote has a microphone button included, along with fast forward, play and rewind buttons.

- It has been designed to be easy to use as well as set up. The elderly and non-techies can set it up, and start using immediately. Adding to the convenience is that registered Amazon account holders, can log in directly through Fire TV. Allowing the user to seamlessly jump right into shows that they are currently watching, and ones that have been marked for future use without the delay of the system having to learn the user's preferences. Set up is very simple, however you would need to buy the HDMI cable needed for set up separately. You then literally plug and play to see your Prime-Time favorites, queue and watch list and all in a matter of minutes.

- Perfect for someone who doesn't have the patience for fiddling with input and output connectors, and all the other confusing cables typically required. Once you have connected your TV to your home Wi-Fi network, you are able to access thousands of free TV episodes and movies that Prime membership offers. This connection is instant and includes being connected to music as well as games.

- The display is crisp and clear, offering a 1080p picture while leaving all default settings intact. Naturally you are able to make adjustments to the sound or video quality, and that can be done in System Settings. While the option to make these changes is possible, there aren't a lot of adjustments that you can make. Resolution settings can be set to either 1080p or 720p at 60 or 50 Hz, but you can calibrate the display so that it scales to fit the size of your screen.

- The earlier mentioned voice search is functional and very good. It is currently the only streaming media device with a voice search function. Simply hold the voice search button and speak. The browsing options appear on the left hand side of the screen, but the user can search easily by speaking into the microphone.

- In addition to Amazon's Prime Instant Video Streaming service, you will be able to watch video content from all of the popular video sharing sites such as Netflix,

YouTube and many more. While HBO GO is not included in this list at present, it is rumored that it will be added sometime toward the end of 2014.

- As mentioned previously, an exclusive feature to the Fire TV device is ASAP, this is short for Advanced Streaming and Prediction. Like the name suggests, it predicts what movies and TV episodes you want to watch, and buffers them for playback long before you reach for the play button.

- The interface is similar to that of the Kindle Fire, with the top column of the Home section showing your recent items, as well as what you have watched and which apps you have used. This makes the interface very user friendly with the intuitive, smooth and responsive functionality.

- With the dedicated Graphic Processing Unit (or graphics card), Fire TV is great for gaming. Allowing you to play all of the current popular games like Minecraft and Asphalt without a glitch. This feature allows the device to be a high quality casual gaming experience, without needing to switch set ups or change connections. Amazon has combined everything that you love about other streaming media boxes, while adding a few surprises of it's own to

Fire TV. Easier and affordable gaming option is one such surprise.

- Users are able to stream live news and sports channels, along with being able to fling any content from the Kindle Fire Tab or Android Smart Phone and watch it on the big screen.

- Another online property that Amazon has integrated into the system is the Internet Movie Database (IMBd), which allows viewers to browse through details of the film they are watching, while they are watching it. This feature is known as XRAY, and using feature gives you access to seeing all the information about the celebrities on your screen. It works as a partner feature with your tablet or smart phone. Kindle Fire HD or HDX users are able to use their device as a second screen for a fuller experience. Simply put, while you are watching Amazon content on your TV, you can use your tablet to check the profiles of characters and actors during a certain scene.

- The all cast screen mirroring feature allows the user to watch all the content saved on their Android Smartphone or Amazon Kindle tablet, on their television. To mirror your screen go to Settings – Display & Sounds – Display Mirroring. Your Kindle

Fire HDX will find the Fire TV Similar to Airplay and displays exactly what you are doing on your smart device. This is a useful feature for presentations, playing games or sharing media with your friends. The option to stream your photographs has been an Apple TV feature for years, however you will be able to store your content on Amazon's Cloud Drive. This Cloud Drive comes with 5GB of storage space with an Amazon Account, but extra space is available and can be purchased if need be. You can view everything that has been saved to the Cloud Drive by going to the Photos section. You can also then change your screensaver to a picture of your choice by going into Settings and changing that there.

- Fire TV is capable of streaming videos and images from Macs and PC's as well as from any Android device. Additionally you can send the video to the big screen by tapping the AirPlay icon at the bottom of the screen, while you watch movies from Amazon on your Kindle Fire HDX.

- Users who are already signed up to Amazon or Amazon Prime, have the added advantage of having access to a lot of free content and apps.

- Amazon has used the Free Time feature from the Kindle Fire tablets for the big screen. It allows you to create a custom environment for children between the ages of 3 and 8, with password protection needed to access other content. The Free Time function is available to Prime Members for an unlimited subscription amount for $2.99. Users can then allow access for their children to all programming suited to their age group.

- Although the build in storage capacity is limited to 8GB, you can use additional storage by using an external hard drive that can be connected to the USB Port. Fire TV also has the added bonus of enabling users to send photos from their iOS device straight to the big screen. These photos will need to be stored on the earlier mentioned Cloud Drive. You can add pictures from your computer using a browser, and then simply drag the files into the Cloud Drive window. Alternatively, users can add photos from their Android, iOS or Kindle Fire devices by downloading the mobile Cloud Drive application.

- As mentioned earlier, the Fire TV system includes a YouTube application that you can use to stream videos from your Android or iOS device. All you would need to do is launch the app on your device and then tap the "cast" icon.

Even with an impressive stream of features, Amazon TV does come with its own set of drawbacks. Let's investigate the "cons" more:

The Cons

- For access for Amazon's Prime Video content library, Amazon Prime customers pay $99. While this does give users the first month of Prime access free, they will be required to pay separately for the same service after the first 13 months subscription is finished.

- Fire TV costs $99 with the TV game controller costing $39.99, which is sold separately. Many people would possibly want to buy them together, but at present there is no package deal available.

- The HDMI cable is sold separately.

- Although the internal storage space is 8GB, 3GB of that is used up already. Leaving only 5GB available for storage.

- Out of the box Android flexibility is limited by the stringent Amazon interface.

- The Fire TV device is strictly a casual gaming machine, even with the ample graphics and sizable 2GB of RAM memory. So users wanting to play games that would use the 2GB of RAM would take up a quarter of the available storage space.

- Although the home screen does have a "recently used" section, showing the last apps the user has used. But there is no option to customize the home screen, so users won't be able to pin their favorite applications or games to the home screen.

- Conventional IR-Based Universal Remotes don't work with Fire TV.

- The price tag is a lot more than what Chrome Cast is charging. Fire TV is priced at $99 while Chrome Cast beats the competition with a $35 price tag.

- According to Amazon, only applications that are Amazon approved will work well on TV. This means that third party apps can't be downloaded or used on Fire TV.

- There is no search engine feature available on Fire TV, so users still have to search each video channel separately to find what they are looking for. At present, there is no way to look for a particular show or movie across all of the channels you can stream on the device.

Like what you've read? Get the rest of the book by scanning this code to download it on Amazon Kindle today!

Look inside ↓

kindle edition

REFERENCES

http://external-battery-charger.com/

http://www.amazon.com/6000mAh-Portable-External-Technology-Smartphones/product-reviews/B00EF1OGOG

http://www.amazon.com/Dual-Port-Compact-External-Battery-Portable/product-reviews/B009USAJCC/ref=dpx_acr_txt?showViewpoints=1

http://lifehacker.com/most-popular-external-battery-pack-anker-astro-series-510076495

http://solarizens.com/review-anker-astro-e5-15000mah dual-usb-portable-charger

http://solarizens.com/anker-astro-mini-3000mah-ultra-compact-lipstick-sized-external-battery-review

http://www.extendedbatteryreview.com/power-banks-external-batteries/anker-astro-mini-3000mah-ultra-compact-portable-charger-lipstick-sized-external-battery-power-bank

http://www.amazon.com/Astro-Ultra-Compact-Lipstick-Sized-Technology-Smartphones/dp/B005X1Y7I2

http://www.ianker.com/support-c7-g345.html

http://9to5mac.com/2014/02/15/review-anker-iq-40w-5-port-smart-usb-adapter-is-the-last-power-source-youll-ever-need/

http://solarizens.com/review-anker-40w-5-port-family-sized-desktop-usb-charger

Disclaimer

All attempts have been made to verify the information contained in this book but the authors and publisher do not bear any responsibility for errors or omissions. Any perceived negative connotation of any individual, group, or company is purely unintentional. Furthermore, this book is intended as a guide and as such, any and all responsibility for actions taken upon reading this book lies with the reader alone and not with the author or publisher. Additionally, it is the reader's responsibility alone and not the author's or publisher's to ensure that all applicable laws and regulations for business practice are adhered to. Lastly, we sometimes utilize affiliate links in the content of this book and as such, if you make a purchase through these links, we will gain a small commission. We have used each of the services listed in this book, however, and as such we can say that we would recommend them to our closest friends with the same ease that we now recommend them to you.

www.ingramcontent.com/pod-product-compliance
Lightning Source LLC
Chambersburg PA
CBHW070903070326
40690CB00009B/1974